Zippy th

Zippy had walked a long distance
in the African savannah to reach a small lake.

He eagerly quenched his thirst
and went to rest under the cool
shade of a baobab tree.

Zippy tried to fall asleep,
but he felt uncomfortable
and very itchy.

For days, there had been tiny fleas
all over his body.

He tried to get rid of the fleas
by swishing his tail from side to side.

He tried to get rid of the fleas
by thumping his four legs
one by one on the ground.

He even tried thumping
all four legs at once!

He rubbed his whole body
against the tree trunk.

He tried to get rid of some fleas
by licking his face
with his long tongue.

But nothing seemed to work!
The fleas just wouldn't go away!

No swishing or licking,
and no rubbing and thumping,
could make them leave him.

Finally, he became so tired and irritated
that he rolled on the ground
with his feet up in the air.

He saw two little birds
perched on a branch
of the mighty baobab.

They made a lot of noise,
winked at each other
and darted down.

"Wow, that was something.
Are you O.K., Pick?"

"Sure, Peck, I'm fine! Ehh- hi, I'm Pick!"
"And I am Peck, hi!"

With a sheepish smile,
Zippy got to his feet.
"Ahem, nice to meet you. I am Zippy."

"You have such deliciously
tempting fleas on you!"
Pick and Peck settled down
on Zippy's back.

"Delicious?" groaned Zippy,
"I am totally bugged by them!
I just can't get them off,
no matter how hard I try."

"We are very hungry, Zippy,
and we love fleas.
May we eat up all these…
nasty creatures?"
asked Pick and Peck.
"Sure! Be my guests!"
exclaimed Zippy delighted.

The birds began.
They pecked at the fleas
on his face and legs,
they cleaned Zippy's belly
and cleaned Zippy's back.

The zebra stood still,
letting the birds eat their fill.

And finally, they were all happy.
The zebra had been freed
of the annoying fleas
and the two birds
had enjoyed a splendid meal.

"Thank you very much
for pecking those nasty fleas off my body."

"Oh! We must thank you,
for providing us with such
a flea meal – free meal."

Animals helping each other –
as Pick and Peck helped Zippy –
is called symbiosis.

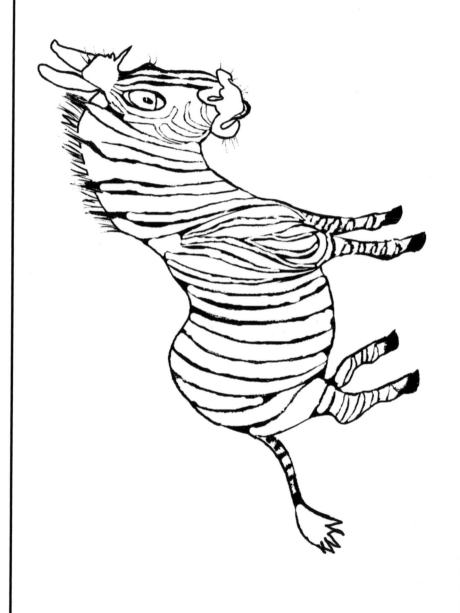

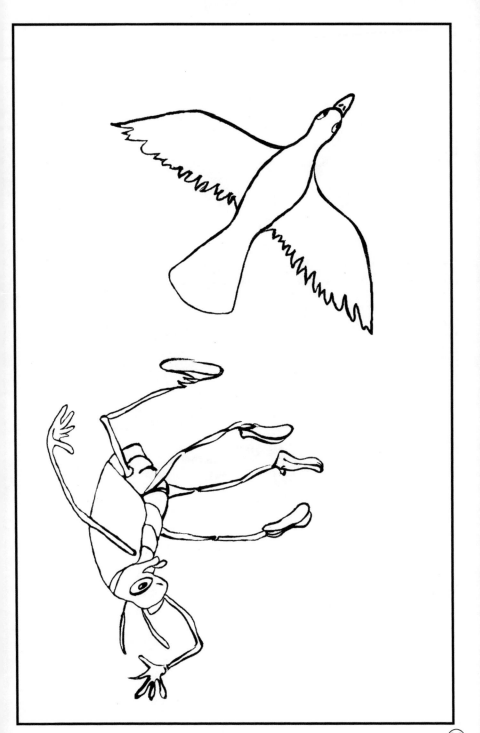

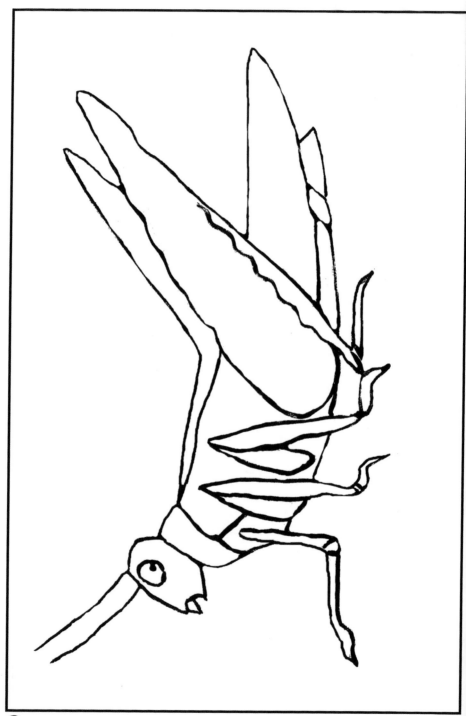

About BookBox

BookBox is a social enterprise with the mission of creating a 'book' for every child in his/her language. In our conception, a 'book' is a reading experience that can travel any audio-visual media platform, including print. We, therefore, innovated the 'AniBook' or animated book, to support early reading and language skills. Visit **www.bookbox.com** to know more.

AniBooks flow from a simple fact – children love to watch cartoons. Thus, AniBooks are animated stories for children, with the narration appearing on-screen as Same Language Subtitles (SLS).

Every word is highlighted in perfect timing with the audio narration, thus reinforcing reading skills, automatically and subconsciously.

SLS is a pedagogically sound and proven technique, which has won many international awards. It has also been implemented widely on film song based TV programs in India, in 10 languages, by our partner non-profit, **www.planetread.org.**

Best Content
DVD Awards
Foundation, India

First Place Winner,
KIDS FIRST!
USA

Winner, Dr. Toy's
Ten Best Audio-Video
Products, USA

Follow us on:

 youtube.com/bookboxinc

 facebook.com/BookBox

 twitter.com/BookBoxInc

Also available on:

 For iPhone & iPad

 For Android

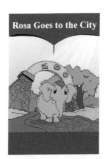

Rosa Goes to the City

Follow the trails of runaway Rosa, a baby elephant loose in the city.

The Four Friends

Animal friends from the "Panchatantra" work together to outwit a hunter and protect the forest!

The Whispering Palms

A delightful story of little Mori who wants her family to live in harmony with nature.

The Boo in the Shoe

Have you ever seen Boos? Discover these magical creatures with Meera.

The Little Pianist

Azul is afraid to perform in front of a crowd. Can a butterfly help?

The First Well

Follow a warrior in search of water to save his people.

Turtle's Flute

Turtle, a gifted flutist, is trapped by a greedy man. How will she escape now?

Tucket the Bucket

Tucket is a sad bucket with a hole. Watch him become the garden favorite again.

Visit www.bookbox.com for stories in over thirty languages.

Printed in Great Britain
by Amazon.co.uk, Ltd.,
Marston Gate.